Historical Disasters

Galveston Hurricane of 1900

by Julie Murray

3

Dash!
LEVELED READERS
An Imprint of Abdo Zoom • abdobooks.com

Dash!
LEVELED READERS

Level 1 – Beginning
Short and simple sentences with familiar words or patterns for children who are beginning to understand how letters and sounds go together.

Level 2 – Emerging
Longer words and sentences with more complex language patterns for readers who are practicing common words and letter sounds.

Level 3 – Transitional
More developed language and vocabulary for readers who are becoming more independent.

THIS BOOK CONTAINS RECYCLED MATERIALS

abdobooks.com

Published by Abdo Zoom, a division of ABDO, PO Box 398166, Minneapolis, Minnesota 55439.

Printed in the United States of America, North Mankato, Minnesota.
052023
092023

Photo Credits: AP Images, Getty Images, Shutterstock
Production Contributors: Kenny Abdo, Jennie Forsberg, Grace Hansen, John Hansen
Design Contributors: Candice Keimig, Neil Klinepier

Library of Congress Control Number: 2022947152

Publisher's Cataloging in Publication Data

Names: Murray, Julie, author.
Title: Galveston hurricane of 1900 / by Julie Murray
Description: Minneapolis, Minnesota : Abdo Zoom, 2024 | Series: Historical disasters | Includes online resources and index.
Identifiers: ISBN 9781098281229 (lib. bdg.) | ISBN 9781098281922 (ebook) | ISBN 9781098282271 (Read-to-me ebook)
Subjects: LCSH: Disasters--Juvenile literature. | History--Juvenile literature. | Hurricanes--Juvenile literature. | Galveston Island (Tex.)--Juvenile literature.
Classification: DDC 976.41--dc23

Table of Contents

Galveston Hurricane of 1900

The Galveston Hurricane of 1900 was the deadliest natural disaster in US history. More than 6,000 lives were lost.

Galveston is a city on Galveston Island, Texas. This **barrier island** sits about 45 miles (72.4 km) southeast of Houston, Texas.

The people of Galveston were not prepared for the storm. Today, there are systems to track storms and alert people in its path. This kind of technology did not exist in 1900.

The Storm

Galveston was a bustling town with about 38,000 residents. All that changed on September 8, 1900, when a category 4 hurricane hit.

At around 8:00 p.m. the storm struck the city. Winds reached speeds up to 140 mph (225 kph).

A **storm surge** pushed ashore by the hurricane's winds washed over the city.

The storm lasted for hours! Many drowned. Some were killed by flying **debris**.

The storm caused great destruction. There was damage to every structure in the city. More than 7,000 buildings were destroyed and 10,000 people were left without a place to live.

The Aftermath

The city worked to rebuild after the storm. More than 2,000 structures were built. Sand was pumped in from the Gulf of Mexico. This helped to raise the island's **elevation** and prevent future disasters.

A seawall was also built. The first **segment** was 3.3 miles (5.3 km) long. More segments have been added over the years. Today, it stretches 10 miles (16 km) long.

More Facts

- The storm is also known as the Great Galveston hurricane and the Great Storm of 1900.
- The hurricane caused $35.4 million in damage. Today, that would equal $1.25 billion!
- A memorial was built in 2000. It marked the storm's 100th anniversary. It is a bronze statue of a family clinging together.

Glossary

barrier island – a long, broad, sandy island lying parallel to a shore that is built up by the action of waves, currents, etc.

debris – scattered pieces left after something has been destroyed.

elevation – the height to which something rises or is raised, or its height above sea level or ground level.

segment – each of the parts into which something may be divided.

storm surge – a rising sea as a result of changes to pressure in the atmosphere and wind associated with a storm.

Index

Online Resources

Booklinks
NONFICTION NETWORK
FREE! ONLINE NONFICTION RESOURCES

To learn more about the Galveston hurricane of 1900, please visit **abdobooklinks.com** or scan this QR code. These links are routinely monitored and updated to provide the most current information available.